THUCYDIDES

ANCIENT GREEK HISTORIAN

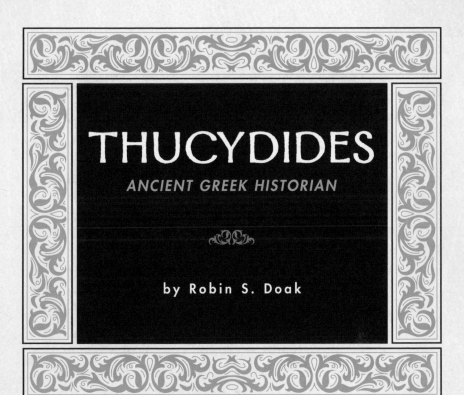

THUCYDIDES
ANCIENT GREEK HISTORIAN

by Robin S. Doak

Content Adviser: Martha Taylor, Ph.D.,
Chair, Department of Classics,
Loyola College in Maryland

Reading Adviser: Rosemary Palmer, Ph.D.,
Department of Literacy, College of Education,
Boise State University

COMPASS POINT BOOKS  MINNEAPOLIS, MINNESOTA

Compass Point Books
3109 West 50th Street, #115
Minneapolis, MN 55410

Visit Compass Point Books on the Internet at *www.compasspointbooks.com*
or e-mail your request to *custserv@compasspointbooks.com*

Editors: Anthony Wacholtz and Julie Gassman
Page Production: Noumenon Creative
Photo Researcher: Svetlana Zhurkin
Cartographer: XNR Productions, Inc.
Library Consultant: Kathleen Baxter

Art Director: Jaime Martens
Creative Director: Keith Griffin
Editorial Director: Carol Jones
Managing Editor: Catherine Neitge

Library of Congress Cataloging-in-Publication Data
Doak, Robin S. (Robin Santos), 1963–
  Thucydides: Ancient Greek Historian / by Robin S. Doak.
      p. cm.—(Signature lives)
  Includes bibliographical references and index.
  ISBN-13: 978-0-7565-1875-2 (hardcover)
  ISBN-10: 0-7565-1875-X (hardcover)
  1. Thucydides—Juvenile literature. 2. Thucydides. History of the
Peloponnesian War—Juvenile literature. 3. Greece—History—
Peloponnesian War, 431–404 B.C.—Historiography—Juvenile literature.
4. Historians—Greece—Biography—Juvenile literature. I. Title. II. Series.
  DF229.T6D63 2007
  938'.05092—dc22   2006003001

Signature Lives

ANCIENT GREECE

After the fall of Troy around 1180 B.C. in the Trojan War, soldiers returned to a Greece mired in famine and economic collapse. It was a time for rebuilding. Greece underwent a political and cultural transformation 400 years after the war with the transition to independent city-states and the establishment of the Olympics. Athens became the hub for developments in architecture, art, science, and philosophy. In about 460 B.C., ancient Greece entered its golden age, one that would produce the establishment of democracy, the beginnings of university study, great strides in medicine and science, architectural advancements, and the creation of plays and epic poems that are still enjoyed today.

Table of Contents

THUCYDIDES.

1 Chapter

LIVING HISTORY, MAKING HISTORY

❧◦◦◦◦❧

Thucydides stood on the deck of a ship and studied the chaos in the small town of Amphipolis that lay before him. Although he commanded part of the world's most powerful navy, he could not prevent the Spartans from capturing the Athenian colony of Amphipolis. On this cold December day in 424 B.C., Thucydides watched helplessly as the Spartan army swarmed over the town's walls. How had this happened? What would become of him once his failure was reported back in Athens?

The Athenian navy had been beaten. As the general assigned to defend the city, Thucydides knew that he must bear the responsibility for the defeat. He also knew the punishment he would receive: either a death sentence or exile from Athens.

Considering Thucydides' privileged past, it was surprising he faced this troubling predicament. A wealthy man and a citizen of one of the most powerful empires in the world, Thucydides had enjoyed an ideal childhood. He had even survived the Great Plague in 430, one of the worst epidemics ever to hit Athens. After being elected as one of Athens' 10 *strategoi*, or generals, his future seemed bright.

Because few official records from Thucydides' time exist, it is impossible to go back and accurately research his life. To create a history of Thucydides—and other ancient Greeks—scholars must carefully read the works of historians and writers who came later, looking for stories about the man that were passed down from those who might have known him. Then they must use their knowledge to determine which stories might be accurate and which ones are probably untrue.

But now, that was all behind him. If he returned to Athens, Thucydides would face the wrath of Greek officials and citizens alike. Instead, he went into exile. Some historians believe that he faced a trial and was sentenced to his exile. Others believe that he may have chosen this punishment before a more severe penalty—death— could be chosen for him.

Now banished from Athens, how would Thucydides spend the coming years? When the Peloponnesian War between Athens and Sparta began seven years earlier, in 431, Thucydides had started writing a history of the battle. Although he was now no longer involved in the actual fighting, he would continue

Peloponnesian War battles were fought on both land and sea. Athens' navy was victorious in a battle near Corinth in 430.

writing about the conflict that had drawn in all of Greece. He visited battlefields and talked to survivors and soldiers from both sides. As long as he stayed away from Athens, he was allowed to travel to other parts of the world.

During his 20 years of exile, Thucydides labored over his work, *The History of the Peloponnesian War*. His retelling of the war was unlike any history ever written before. Thucydides was the first person to record events as they were happening. He was also one of the first people to interview those who helped make history. While other historians wrote about events of the past, Thucydides tried to report

THUCYDIDES

WITH AN ENGLISH TRANSLATION BY
CHARLES FORSTER SMITH
OF THE UNIVERSITY OF WISCONSIN

IN FOUR VOLUMES
I

HISTORY OF THE PELOPONNESIAN WAR
BOOKS I AND II

LONDON
WILLIAM HEINEMANN LTD
CAMBRIDGE, MASSACHUSETTS
HARVARD UNIVERSITY PRESS
MCMLXII

the Peloponnesian War through the eyes of those who saw it take place. He tried to be accurate and unbiased, even though he was Athenian.

Thucydides did more than just report battles. He analyzed the events of the past to show how they affected the present, and he explored the reasons for the war. He also studied the historic, social, religious, and political causes that resulted in the two great powers of Greece—Athens and Sparta—making war upon each other for 27 years.

Thucydides' undertaking was so colossal that he was unable to cover the entire war before he died. However, his incomplete work changed the way history was written. Today, Thucydides is remembered as the father of scholarly history—the writing of history based on a thorough examination of primary sources, such as letters, official records, and interviews.

Modern historians have used Thucydides' book to gain insight on more recent wars, including World War I (1914–1918), the Cold War (a period of tense rivalry between communist and noncommunist nations), and even the post-9/11 world. Some scholars, for example, have used Thucydides' retelling of Athenian actions to explain modern-day U.S. foreign policy by comparing the United States to Athens.

Thucydides' history also gives modern readers a good look at Athens, the world's first democracy. Today, people know about the politics of this ancient civilization because Thucydides so carefully recorded it.

2 GROWING UP IN GOLDEN ATHENS

❧⟨✦⟩❧

Although he is one of the world's most famous historians, little is known about Thucydides' personal life. He recorded the smallest details about the Peloponnesian War and its causes but did not reveal much about himself. Since his book did not become famous until many years after his death, no one wrote about the historian while he was still alive.

Thucydides did not even record the year he was born. In his history, he said he was a young adult when the war broke out in 431. So historians think that he was born after 460, most likely sometime in the 450s.

Thucydides wrote that he was born in Athens, Greece. At the time of his birth, Athens was one of the largest and most important city-states in ancient Greece. A city-state was an independent state made

Elaborate architecture and art, including a statue of the goddess Athena in the Parthenon, were some of the treasures of ancient Greece's golden age.

Ancient Greece, around 400 B.C.
Present-day Greece boundary

Black
Sea

Thrace

Macedonia

Amphipolis

Illyria

Eion Thasos

Mt. Olympus

Epirus

Hellespont River
(Dardanelles)

Phrygia

Thessaly

Aegean

Lesbos

Delphi

Euboea Sea

ASIA
MINOR

Plataea Thebes

Gulf of Corinth

Attica Marathon

Olympia

Corinth

Athens

Peloponnesus

Argos

Miletus

Naxos

Halicarnassus

Sparta

Melos

Rhodes

N
W   E
S

0   90 miles

0   90 kilometers

Crete

Mediterranean Sea

*Among the
most powerful
city-states were
Athens, Sparta,
and Corinth.*

up of a strong city and the surrounding towns and
territories that depended upon it. At this time, Greece
was made up of several hundred independent city-
states. The territory included present-day Greece as
well as colonies in southern Italy; the Greek islands;
and along the coasts of the Aegean, Ionian, and
Black seas. Each city-state, or *polis*, prided itself

on its ability to make its own laws and choose its own government. About 7 million people considered themselves Greek.

Thucydides was born into an aristocratic, or noble, family. His father was Olorus. His name was connected to Thrace, an ancient kingdom in southeastern Europe. Olorus was also the name of a Thracian king, leading some historians to believe that Thucydides may have been descended from a royal family. He may also have been related to Miltiades, the great Athenian general who beat the Persians at the Battle of Marathon in 490 B.C. His mother was named Hegesypule, but little else is known about her. It is not known if he had any brothers or sisters.

Miltiades
(540?–488? B.C.)

Although he was the son of a wealthy nobleman, Thucydides' lifestyle was probably not so different from most Athenian citizens. These people were known for their simple style of living. In the city's crowded, bustling marketplace, one could buy fish, wheat, barley, olives, and fruit imported from Athenian colonies. Athenians kept their own goats for milk and cheese, and many made wine.

Thucydides' home was most likely made of clay bricks baked in the sun. Like other Greek dwellings, his home might have had separate apartments for men and women surrounding an open courtyard. Residents decorated their walls with murals and their floors with tiles and stones. Although there were rooms for cooking and eating, many meals were prepared outside in a brazier, a large metal pan used to hold hot coals. On hot summer nights, many Greeks slept on their roofs to catch a cool breeze.

The home was the women's domain. Women and

Athens' agora was a popular gathering spot.

girls, especially those from wealthy families, spent much of their lives there. They were allowed outside only on special occasions, such as funerals, festivals, and sometimes the theater. When they went out, they had to be accompanied by a male chaperone. When male visitors called on their husbands, wives were expected to stay within their own apartments. Poorer women and female slaves had greater freedom to appear in public. Poorer women sold food, wine, and other goods in the market, called the agora. Slaves, who were often prisoners of war, shopped for their masters, buying food and other household items.

Women in ancient Greece ran all aspects of the household, including preparing food, making clothes, and caring for children. Wealthier families, like Thucydides', might have owned slaves who worked with the women. Girls worked alongside their mothers until they were teenagers. Then they married a man chosen by their fathers.

Like other Greek boys, Thucydides wore the simple fashions popular with Athenians. Both men and women wore long pieces of linen or wool draped around the body and held in place with ribbons or

Ancient Greek fashions were simple items made from one or two rectangular pieces of fabric.

pins. These garments were dyed in various colors. Another style of clothing worn by Athenians was the chiton, a long, sleeveless shirt. A belt tightened the garment at the waist. Sandals covered their feet. In Athens' mild climate, a cloak was usually all that was needed to keep warm on cold days.

Thucydides and other wealthy and noble-born boys had an advantage over commoners and girls— they were given an education. Around the age of 7, boys were sent to a neighborhood school, where male teachers taught them to read and write. As they grew older, they learned math, science, and government. Thucydides, like other boys, was taught to write and debate, two important areas of education at the time.

Physical exercise was essential to all Athenian males. One important gathering place was the gymnasion, an open area where men exercised together. As a boy, Thucydides probably took part in gymnastics, wrestling, and footraces. Later, he was trained to fight and handle weapons, such as a spear.

One place where Greek men

In his book, Thucydides described a traditional Greek hair fashion that was worn by wealthy, older men. Instead of wearing their hair long, as most Athenian men did, these elders wore their hair tied at the back of their heads in a knot. The knot was fastened with a golden clasp shaped like a grasshopper. When Thucydides began writing his history, he said that the old men of Athens had recently given up knotting their hair.

The first recorded Olympic Games were held in 776 B.C. at Olympia with just one event, a running race. When Thucydides lived, the Games were at their peak. Only honorable Greek men could participate in the Games, and, as was the custom, they competed in the nude. Each man participated for his own glory, not for a team or city-state. Married women were not permitted to attend. If a married woman was caught at the Games, she could suffer the ultimate penalty— death. However, Greek women could take part in their own games, the Heraea, held in honor of the goddess Hera, wife of Zeus.

showed off their athletic skills was at the Olympic Games. These athletic contests were held to honor the god Zeus and took place every four years at Olympia, a town west of Athens. The games included chariot racing, wrestling, and bare-knuckles boxing. Winners became celebrities and were honored with gifts and special privileges when they returned home.

The arts were also important to the Athenians. Students were required to memorize poems by the great Greek poets of the day. One of the most famous of these poets, Homer, lived in the eighth century B.C. and composed *The Iliad* and *The Odyssey*, two epics that are still read today. Athenian boys also learned to play the flute or the lyre, an instrument that looked like a small harp.

Thucydides' Athens was the most advanced city of its time. Many spectacular buildings were built during this golden age, including the Parthenon, one of Greece's most famous buildings, which was begun in 447.

The Parthenon was located on top of the Acropolis, a rocky hilltop that was the city's religious and military center. This beautiful, white marble building was a temple to Athena, the goddess of wisdom. A huge wooden statue of Athena, covered with gold and ivory, stood in one of the temple's two big rooms.

The famed Greek poet Homer

Most of the fifth century B.C. is considered Athens' golden age. Although it was a time of war, it was also a time of prosperity and great cultural achievement. Today, when people talk about "classical Greece," they often mean Athens during this period. While we know much more about the era than we do Thucydides himself, we can see how the world he lived in may have shaped his experiences. ❧

ΠΕΡΙΚΛΗΣ

3 THE WORLD'S FIRST DEMOCRACY

❦

Thucydides grew up in the world's first democracy. The word *democracy* comes from the Greek words *demos*, meaning "people," and *kratos*, meaning "rule." Athenians adopted the new political system around 500 B.C., approximately 50 years before Thucydides was born.

Athens had begun slowly moving toward a democratic form of government in 594. Until that time, the city had been governed by kings, groups of aristocrats, or tyrants. In ancient times, the word *tyrant* meant a person, usually an aristocrat, who seized leadership of a city or kingdom for himself. Although some Greek tyrants were harsh rulers, others were popular with the people they ruled.

In 510, the Athenians overthrew a tyrant after a

reign of terror. An aristocrat named Cleisthenes took power and created the first democratic constitution. Until that time, Athenians were only considered citizens if they descended from one of Athens' four original tribes, or groups of families. Under Cleisthenes, all free males over the age of 18 were made citizens.

Cleisthenes divided Athens into districts based on the village a person lived in, rather than the clan to which each person belonged. Each district included both aristocrats and commoners. Every year, representatives from the districts took part in the Council of 500, which Cleisthenes set up to help govern Athens. The representatives were chosen randomly at an annual lottery.

The chief decision-making group in Athens was the Ecclesia, or assembly. The Ecclesia was made up of Athens' citizens. Nearly every week, the group assembled at a huge, open-air auditorium located on a hill west of the Acropolis. Here the Ecclesia listened to proposals made by the Council of 500. Proposals could also be made from the floor by Athenian citizens. After

With the rise of a democracy came professional politicians called demagogues. They were usually excellent and persuasive speakers who often spoke to the Ecclesia to convince Athenian citizens to support them. In ancient Athens, the word demagogue meant "leader of the people." Today, a demagogue is a politician who appeals to people's emotions and prejudices to win an election.

hearing debates on both sides of the issues, citizens voted by raising their hands. In his history, Thucydides wrote of a man named Diodotus, who described the role of speakers and debates in democracy: "The good citizen ought to triumph not by frightening his opponents but by beating them fairly in argument."

Not everyone in Athens had a voice in the new system. Women were not considered citizens and could not participate in the government. People from other countries who lived in Athens could not participate either.

Athens' slaves were also excluded from the Ecclesia. Some Athenian slaves could save money to buy their own freedom. They could even become wealthy and gain political power for themselves. However, former slaves could never become Athenian citizens.

As Athens developed into the world's first democracy, it was also becoming one of Greece's strongest military and political powers. During the wars against Persia that stretched from 499 to 479 B.C., Athens sent military aid to the Greek city-states in Asia Minor that were revolting against Persian rule. In 490, an outnumbered Athenian army defeated the Persian army at the Battle of Marathon. The surprising victory showed the world that the Athenians were a power to be reckoned with. Ten years later, Athens' new navy also proved to be unstoppable. During a sea battle near Salamis, an island right off the coast of Athens, the Athenian navy sank about half of all the Persian ships.

In the following years, the Athenian navy liberated many Greek cities and towns that had been captured by Persia. These towns joined with Athens and other towns to form the Delian League to fight Persia. At its height, the

The Battle of Marathon marked the beginning of the Athenian Empire and left a lasting milestone: the marathon race. After the battle, an Athenian general asked his best runner, Pheidippides, to make the more than 21-mile (33.6-kilometer) journey to Athens to spread news of the victory. Although the young man had just run back to the battlefield from Sparta—150 miles (240 km) away—he agreed. Pheidippides sprinted from Marathon to Athens in about three hours. According to the story, he arrived and delivered the message, "Nik-eh!" or "Victory!" He then collapsed and died. Marathon races are still held today.

At the Battle of Marathon, about 10,000 Athenians defeated 60,000 Persians.

Delian League was made up of about 200 city-states. With its powerful navy, Athens was chosen to lead the league. Other members were expected to send ships, men, or money to keep Athens' navy strong. They could not refuse to take part in any military campaigns that Athens initiated against Persia, and they promised not to fight with one another.

After Greece made peace with Persia in 466, there was no need for the Delian League to continue. However, Athens continued to force league members to send money to support its navy. In later years, the Delian League would be transformed from an alliance against Persia to a powerful Athenian empire.

The new empire earned the resentment of some league members who objected to paying for services they did not need or require. When describing the causes of the Peloponnesian War, Thucydides wrote:

The Treasury of the Athenians at Delphi is a symbol of the wealth and power of Athens in the fifth century B.C.

Of all the causes of defection, that connected with arrears [debts] for tribute and vessels, and with failure of service, was the chief; for the Athenians were very severe and exacting.

To keep hold of their power in the face of such resentment, Athenians worked to establish democratic governments in these cities. They believed democracies would remain loyal to Athens.

One of the strongest supporters of democracy in Athens and the rest of Greece was a man named Pericles. Born to a noble family in Athens around 490, Pericles was the great-nephew of Cleisthenes, founder of Athens' democratic constitution. As a young man, Pericles joined a political group that was devoted to keeping Athens a democracy. About the time Thucydides was born, Pericles was the leader of the group and, as one of Athens' 10 elected generals, one of the most influential men in Athens. In his history, Thucydides described the Athenian politician as "the best man of all for the needs of the state."

Pericles did more than just strengthen Athens' military might. He also made many changes to the Athenian government. Officials were now paid a salary, and poor men were given the same rights as rich men. However, Athenian citizenship became even more exclusive. Only people who could prove Athenian ancestry on both their mother's and father's sides were considered citizens.

Yet under Pericles' leadership, Athens flourished both culturally and economically. The Athenians made great achievements in art, literature, architecture,

Olives were an important product for Greek city-states. The ancient Greeks used olive oil to cook and flavor foods. It was also used to make soap and to fuel their lamps. Olive oil was a major trade item for the Greeks. They exported it to Slavic cities in exchange for grain. Because of the olive's importance, invading armies often destroyed the enemy's olive trees.

and education. The city-state also became an important center of shipping and trade. Athenians exported olive oil, silver, perfumes, and pottery to other Greek city-states. They imported grain, jewelry, and metal goods from Egypt, Slavic cities, and other parts of Greece. During a funeral speech in Thucydides' book, Pericles said:

The magnitude of our city draws the produce of the world into our harbor, so that to the Athenian the fruits of other countries are as familiar a luxury as those of his own.

Beginning in 460 B.C., Pericles oversaw the expansion of the Athenian empire. The skilled orator persuaded Athenian citizens to support taking control of more cities, towns, and regions. He convinced Athenians that their city-state was the most glorious and powerful, saying that Athens should be at the head of a large empire. He pointed out the benefits of being in control, one of which was the money deposited in the Delian League's treasury. These funds eventually helped pay for art and architecture in Athens, in addition to supporting the strong navy.

Athens' wealth also benefited the people directly. Poor common men worked as rowers in the fleet, performed public works around the empire, and even held paid offices. Wealthier citizens no longer had to pay to support Athens' large navy. And both poor and wealthy Athenians were often given large estates or plots of land in other parts of the empire. Wealth from the empire also allowed Athens' democracy to run smoothly. Athenian citizens now had the leisure

The important crop of olives was often depicted on ancient Greek pottery.

On the eve of the *Peloponnesian War*, *Athens'* navy was like none that had ever existed. The 250-ship fleet was made up of warships with three levels of rowers on each side, one above the other. These ships were about 120 feet (36.6 meters) long and 15 feet (4.6 m) wide. Their small size made them faster than other ships of the time and much easier to maneuver. As many as 174 rowers worked on each ship, along with the captain, 25 officers, and a handful of archers and spearmen. Each ship was equipped with a bronze-covered ram that was used to destroy other enemy ships by running into them.

time needed to serve on the council and on juries.

In time, more than 250 towns came under Athenian control. Many were happy to be part of Athens' new empire. Their citizens were hired to help man the Athenian navy. These men, in turn, returned home and spent their wages, which boosted the local economy. Member towns were given protection by the powerful Athenian navy for less money than it would cost to build and maintain their own ships.

As Athens prospered, Thucydides matured into a young man. His aristocratic birth allowed him to move into influential circles. He met people who were making history during one of Athens' most important times. He may have attended symposia, or dinner sessions, where drink and conversation flowed freely. Here he would have heard people like Pericles who supported democracy, as well as those who opposed it.

Like most Athenian men, Thucydides probably got married when he was 18 or older. In Athens,

boys completed their education and became citizens at this age. While historians are not certain he wed, some believe he did and that his wife may have been from Thrace.

Around this time, Thucydides was given an estate in Thrace by either his father or his wife. This second home was at Scapte Hyle, a small town located along Thrace's coast. In ancient times, Scapte Hyle was a center of gold mining, and Thucydides later wrote that he owned a gold mine. Although he didn't realize it yet, Thucydides' second home would one day provide him with a much-needed shelter. ✍

4 THE ROOTS OF WAR

❧

Much of what we know about Thucydides comes from studying his work, *The History of the Peloponnesian War*. This written history, consisting of eight volumes, is important because it focused not only on the events of the Peloponnesian War but also on the reasons the conflict started. The historian carefully chronicled the rise of the Athenian empire and the growing anxiety of the Greek city-states that were not allied with Athens. Although these events occurred several years before Thucydides was born, he knew they were important areas to explore if his history was to be fully understood.

According to Thucydides, one city-state that was especially worried was the small town of Sparta in southern Greece. Sparta was the chief city-state

Prepared for battle, Spartan hoplites, or foot soldiers, wore a helmet and armor and armed themselves with a spear, shield, and sword.

37

The city-state of Sparta lay in southern Greece.

of an empire that stretched over the Peloponnesus on Greece's southern peninsula. The empire was commonly called the Peloponnesian League or the Spartan Alliance. It was made up of city-states that had signed treaties with Sparta.

The city-states of the Peloponnesian League were treated fairly by Sparta. When councils were held, each city-state, including Sparta, got one vote. Sparta let other members keep their own independence. And, as Thucydides pointed out, the Spartans did not ask for any tribute. The city-state had no desire to expand its own empire.

Unlike democratic Athens, Sparta and other members of the Peloponnesian League were oligarchies, governments run by groups of high-born men. In Thucydides' book, an Athenian leader named Athenagoras described the difference between the two types of government:

> It will be said, perhaps, that democracy is neither wise nor equitable, but that the holders of property are also the best fitted to rule. I say, on the contrary ... that the word demos, or people, includes the whole state, oligarchy only a part.

Another difference between the two city-states was in their military might. Whereas Athens had forged an empire by being a naval power, Sparta was a land power. Their army was one of the largest and best in the world. From the age of 7, Spartan boys were trained to be part of Sparta's military. Most Greeks believed that Sparta's trained army was unbeatable.

Although Sparta and Athens

Spartan women had more rights and privileges than other women in ancient Greece. Girls in Sparta were taught to read and write and could take part in musical competitions, gymnastics, and footraces. After they married, women not only ran their own households but could also own businesses and property. Spartan women were expected to be physically fit, bear healthy children, and defend their homes when their husbands were away. Their loyalty to Sparta came before everything else, even their family. It is said that one Spartan mother told her son before battle, "Come home with your shield or dead upon it."

Education in Sparta concentrated on physical strength and agility.

fought together against Persia, mistrust and suspicion arose between them once the wars were over. Sparta had been the most powerful city-state in all of Greece, but as Athens grew stronger with each passing day, Spartan officials decided to act.

The first conflict between Athens and Sparta began when Athenians started to rebuild city walls that had been destroyed by Persian troops. Sparta immediately objected. With strong, new walls, Athens would be even more powerful. Since Greece and Persia were no longer fighting, the Spartans wondered why Athens needed to rebuild its walls. According to Thucydides, an embassy of Spartans traveled to Athens to try to convince the Athenians to stop the construction. The Athenians ignored Sparta's complaints and made the walls bigger and better than before.

Another city-state that resented Athens' growing power was Corinth. Located 50 miles (80 km) to the west of Athens, wealthy Corinth was a major center of trade and shipping. The city, surrounded by fertile farmland, was also an important agricultural center. The Corinthians resented the success of their neighbors to the east. When Athens openly supported some of Corinth's rebellious colonies, the relationship between the two city-states became hostile.

In the years leading up to the Peloponnesian War, Corinth strongly encouraged Sparta to attack and destroy Athens. According to Thucydides, the Corinthians spoke

After the Peloponnesian War, Corinth would never again enjoy the success it had once had. In 338 B.C., the city was conquered by Philip of Macedonia, father of Alexander the Great. In 146 B.C., Corinth was destroyed by the Romans but was later rebuilt by Julius Caesar as a Roman colony. By 1458, the once-powerful city was merely a small town under Turkish rule. Four hundred years later, Corinth was again destroyed, this time by an earthquake. Today, modern Corinth lies three miles (4.8 km) northeast of the ancient city.

to the Spartans with these words: "We have very great complaints of the high-handed treatment by the Athenians and of neglect by you."

Even some of Athens' allies were unhappy with the new Athenian empire of which they were a part. They resented the city's growing control over them. As time went on, Athens became more powerful and less willing to listen to its allies. Athenian officials began taking money and supplies without asking permission from the other league members.

Some league members wanted their independence back and didn't want to pay tribute to Athens. Thucydides wrote that the first member to try to leave the Delian League was the island of Naxos. In the 460s B.C., Naxos islanders rebelled against Athenian authority. The island was soon visited by Cimon, Athens' greatest general, and a fleet of ships. The people of Naxos quickly surrendered.

Other towns that tried to rise up against Athens suffered the same fate. Rebellious towns lost more of their freedom, even

Cimon, Athenian general

their ability to choose and run their own govern-ments. Towns were forced to give up their navies and accept a democratic government. They were also required to pay tribute to Athens in cash, which was difficult for many towns and lessened the chances that the cash-strapped communities could fund future rebellions.

Around 465, before Thucydides was born, the division between Athens and Sparta grew wider. The island of Thasos revolted against Athenian rule. Officials in Thasos sent messages to Sparta asking for help. They hoped the powerful city-state would attack Attica, the district in east-central Greece of which Athens was a part. The people in Thasos believed that such an attack would take Athens' attention away from their island. Thucydides said that Sparta planned to assist Thasos until a violent earthquake shook the city, causing death and destruction. Following the big quake, Sparta's slaves, the helots, rose up against the rest of the city. These slaves made up the largest segment of Sparta's population. At the time of the Peloponnesian War, they

Sparta's economy relied heavily on the labor of its huge population of state-owned slaves called helots. Most helots were farm-workers forced to labor in their masters' fields with little or no reward. Spartans lived in constant fear of slave rebellions. Because Spartans feared their helots, slaves were not part of the early fighting forces. Instead, helots often went along in battle as servants to Spartan soldiers. As the Peloponnesian War dragged on, however, Spartan generals began using helots as soldiers.

outnumbered Spartan citizens 7-to-1.

Sparta was forced to request help from other city-states. Athens, like other cities, sent troops to help end the revolt. However, Spartan officials told the Athenians that their help was not needed. No other city-state was treated this way, and Sparta's snub of Athens caused bitter feelings between the two powerful empires. In his history, Thucydides later wrote that "the first open quarrel between the Spartans and Athenians arose out of this expedition."

Sparta sat on the Peloponnesus, an 8,300-square-mile (21,580-sq-km) peninsula in southern Greece.

Back home in Athens, hatred of the Spartans increased. When the rebellious helots were permitted to safely leave Sparta as long as they never returned, Athens stepped in to help. The Athenians settled the rebellious men and women in the city of Naupactus on the Corinthian Gulf "because of the hatred that [Athens] now felt for the Spartans."

Over the coming years, the rift between Athens and Sparta grew wider. This caused tension throughout Greece. Cities or towns that were angry with one of the two big powers could look to the other as an ally. The entire Greek world began lining up behind either Sparta or Athens.

In 437, Athens founded the colony of Amphipolis, one of the most important of its new settlements. Because of its accessibility to the Aegean Sea, Amphipolis quickly became one of the empire's busiest ports. Located to the south of Greece's richest mining region, Amphipolis also served as an important center of trade and transportation. It would later play an important role in the story of Thucydides and his famous history. ❧

ΘΟΚΥΔΙΔΗΣ

5 THE WAR BEGINS

Chapter

ಲೊ⊰ಎ

Thucydides said that he began writing *The History of the Peloponnesian War* as soon as the war broke out. He thought the conflict "would be a great war, and more worthy of relation than any that had preceded it." He explained his beliefs:

> *Both powers were then at their best in preparedness for war in every way, and seeing the rest of the Hellenic [Greek] people taking sides with one side or the other, some at once, others planning to do so. For this was the greatest upheaval that had ever shaken Hellenes [Greece] also to some part of the barbarians, one might say even to a very large part of mankind.*

For Thucydides, it was important that future

generations have a history of the war. He knew that his book could serve as both a window into the past and a key to understanding future events. In Book I, the first part of his work, he wrote:

> *I shall be content if the future student of these events, or of other similar events which are likely in human nature to occur in after ages, finds my narrative of them useful.*

The causes of the conflict are outlined in Book I. The historian started Book II by writing, "The war between the Athenians and Peloponnesians and the allies on either side now really begins."

In March 431 B.C., 300 men from Thebes, a powerful ally of Sparta, invaded the small democratic city of Plataea. The attack, which was carried out in the dead of night, was a failure. The people of Plataea fought back and captured most of the invaders. Angry over the sneaky, dishonorable night attack, Plataea's citizens executed 180 prisoners, even after promising not to do so. Then they turned to Athens for help.

Although neither Sparta nor Athens was involved in the attack on Plataea, this invasion started the Peloponnesian War. Pericles, the Athenian general, convinced the Athenian assembly to send troops to defend Plataea against future attacks from Thebes. Pericles knew that the move would mean war with

Sparta, yet he convinced the Athenian assembly to go along with his plans.

Years before the invasion of Plataea, Spartans fought against Persians on Plataean soil in 479 B.C.

Because he was an excellent orator, Pericles was able to gather a group of soldiers and politicians who were loyal to him. As a result, the Athenian assembly almost always followed his advice. Thucydides called Pericles "the leading man in Athens at that time and the ablest in speech and in action." He wrote that Athens was "in name a democracy but really a government by the first citizen," referring to Pericles.

Although the attack on Plataea was said to be the cause of the war, Thucydides believed that there were other causes that had been brewing for many years. He wrote:

The truest cause was one not much admitted at the time: it was the growth of Athenian power, which frightened the Spartans and forced them to war.

> In his history, Thucydides does not give much attention to the role women played during the war. One of the rare mentions of Athenian women comes in Book 1, when the historian relates that women and children helped rebuild the wall that protected Athens. He later mentions the wailing of the female relatives at the funerals of those who died during the early days of the Peloponnesian War.

Thucydides' judgment was the first time any writer had attempted to look beneath the surface and find the true cause of a conflict or event. Throughout his writings, Thucydides would discuss the real and stated causes of events.

According to Thucydides, the Spartans believed they were fighting for "freedom for the Greeks." They wanted to break up the Delian League and put an end to Athens' control of their empire. The Spartans knew they would have to destroy Athens' powerful navy—and the city itself. The Spartans believed that their army, the strongest in Greece, was ready for the task.

Most people in Greece believed that Sparta's army could force Athens to its knees in a year or two. The Peloponnesian War, however, would drag on for 27 bloody years. One of the most vicious ever fought, the long war was the cause of many violent acts, especially in later years. Innocent citizens were killed or sold into slavery. Entire cities were destroyed. Thucydides wrote:

> *War takes away the easy supply of daily wants, and so proves a rough master, that brings most men's characters to a level with their fortunes.*

He noted that the harsh conditions of war brought out the worst in many people.

True to what Thucydides thought, the conflict quickly moved from a dispute between two city-states into a war that involved the entire Greek world. City-states chose sides based on their form of government or past alliances. For example, many democracies and members of the Delian League supported Athens. Oligarchies and Peloponnesian League members sided with Sparta and its leader, Archidamus II.

Spartan leader Archidamus II

Towns donated soldiers and funds to their allies. Sparta had more difficulty raising money for supplies and troops. Unlike Athens, the city had no tribute. But Sparta's allies did what they could. One

The Greek city-states allied with either Sparta or Athens.

donation, for example, was a gift of raisins.

During the first year of the war, Sparta invaded Attica and destroyed fields of grain, grapevines, and olive trees. They burned houses and other buildings. Although many Athenians wanted revenge, Pericles encouraged them to be patient. Athens' army was no match for the great army of the Peloponnesian League. Pericles moved people living outside Athens into the city for protection. Other people living in Attica moved to nearby islands to be safe. The Athenian leader had decided that the best strategy at this time was to defend themselves against Spartan attacks.

At first, Athenians strongly supported the defensive war against Sparta and its allies. But crowded conditions within Athens soon led to frustration. People from outside of Athens wanted to be back in their own homes, and Athenians wanted them out of the city. When Spartan troops advanced within a few miles of Athens, the anger of the people exploded.

Pericles was the target of this anger. The people labeled Athens' "first citizen" a coward. They began to question why he was so afraid to attack the Peloponnesian army. The leader of this criticism was Cleon, the son of a Greek tanner. Although Cleon was a commoner with little education, he was a gifted speaker. He had power to inspire those who listened to him, and he used this power to attack Pericles.

Cleon's harsh criticism of Pericles angered those who supported the Greek leader. One person who disliked Cleon was Thucydides. He called Cleon "the most violent man at Athens, and at that time by far the most powerful with the commons." In one section of the book, Thucydides reported the speeches of all the major people involved—except Cleon.

Despite the challenge to his leadership, Pericles was able to continue his method of waging war. After a year of warfare, Athens was still unconquered, and the Peloponnesians had done little damage that could not be repaired. Eventually, the Spartans and their allies returned home with little accomplished.

To honor those who had died in war, it was an Athenian custom to give a public funeral speech at the end of the first year of battle. Although the people

Many people came to listen to the funeral speech delivered by Pericles.

had been angry with Pericles, they chose him to give this important speech. Thucydides included Pericles' funeral speech in Book II of his history. It is the most famous part of *The History of the Peloponnesian War* and one of the most famous speeches ever written. Some modern-day scholars have even suggested that the speech influenced President Abraham Lincoln when he was writing his famous Gettysburg Address.

In the speech, Pericles talked first about Athens and democracy:

> *We do not copy our neighbors: rather, we are an example to them. Our system is called a democracy, for it respects the majority and not the few; but while the law secures equality to all alike in their private disputes, the claim of excellence is also recognized.*

Pericles also reminded Athenians about their duty to take an active role in the government. Pericles believed that an Athenian who neglected to take part in the city's democracy—either by voting or by speaking—was not a good citizen:

> *Our public men have, besides politics, their private affairs to attend to, and our ordinary citizens, though occupied with other pursuits of industry, are still*

For centuries, scholars have tried to determine which writers might have influenced Thucydides. Some historians believe that two influences may have been the great Greek playwrights Sophocles and Euripides. Both writers excelled at tragedies, dramatic plays with unhappy endings. Sophocles, who also served as an Athenian general in 440 B.C., wrote 123 plays. However, only seven of these works still exist in complete form. Euripides' works were less popular than those of Sophocles. Like his fellow playwright, few of Euripides' works survived. Of the 90 plays he is thought to have penned, only 19 still exist.

fair judges of public matters. For unlike any other nation, we regard the citizen who takes no part in these duties not as unambitious but as useless.

Finally, Pericles talked about the meaning of true freedom and why Athenians needed to continue to support his manner of fighting the Spartans. He said, "Judging happiness to be the fruit of freedom and freedom of valor, never decline the dangers of war."

It is unlikely that these words were the exact ones spoken by Pericles himself. It is more likely that they were mostly the invention of Thucydides. Throughout his book, Thucydides put words into the mouths of many important figures. There are 40 speeches in *The History of the Peloponnesian War*, and they make up about one-fourth of the entire work. All of the speeches are written in Thucydides' style. He never revealed his exact sources, so historians don't know whether he witnessed a speech or someone else told him about it.

Thucydides used the speeches as a way to describe what was going on at the moment. These speeches reveal many things about the events of the war. They also reveal what Thucydides thought about the speaker. He did not reserve much space in his book for people he did not like. He admitted that he used these speeches to make a point:

> *With reference to the speeches in this history, some were delivered before the war began, others while it was going on; some I heard myself, others I got from various quarters; it was in all cases difficult to carry them word for word in one's memory, so my habit has been to make the speakers say what was in my opinion demanded of them by the various occasions, of course adhering as closely as possible to the general sense of what they really said.*

Today, credible historians would not consider putting words into the mouths of historical figures. Centuries after Thucydides' death, recording devices and reporting practices made getting exact quotes possible. But in Thucydides' time, oral histories, which always bore the imprint of the teller, were heavily relied upon to pass down events as or after they happened. ✍

Chapter

6 THE GREAT PLAGUE

༼ꗰꗰꗰꗰ༽

In May 430 B.C., when Thucydides was a young man in his 20s, King Archidamus of Sparta invaded Attica again. In the coming weeks, Sparta's army attacked cities and towns near Athens and along the coast. Safe behind their strong city walls, the Athenians refused to budge or challenge Sparta's army on land. After 40 days, the Spartans ran out of supplies and returned home.

With the Spartans gone, life in Athens returned to normal. But, in the early days of summer, disaster struck. People inside the city began falling ill with a mysterious and deadly disease. Few people recovered from the illness. The first sign of the disease was a high fever, followed by coughing and labored breathing. During the final stages of the disease, the

The only surviving record of the plague is Thucydides' work.

infected person's skin became covered with pustules, or pimples, that leaked "bile of every kind named by physicians." Victims of the Great Plague, as the epidemic became known, usually suffered about seven days before dying.

In the cramped and crowded city, the sickness spread quickly from one person to another. To make matters worse, Athens had no sewage system. People threw garbage and human waste into the streets, and slave workers collected it. Even animals became infected. Soon, the epidemic was raging out of control.

The Great Plague raged through Athens for two years. People fled the city, leaving their sick and dying friends or relatives to fend for themselves. The bodies of the dead were thrown in mass graves.

In 429, Thucydides became seriously ill with the plague. After he recovered, he recorded as much information as he could about the Great Plague. In Book II of *The History of the Peloponnesian War*, he discussed the disaster and even tried to trace the epidemic's origins. Thucydides believed that the disease might have been carried into Athens by infected foreign soldiers. He reported that the first outbreak occurred in present-day Ethiopia or Egypt and then spread from there.

Thucydides described the illness as accurately as possible so that "it may be recognized by the student, if it should ever break

When writing his descriptions of the Great Plague, Thucydides may have been influenced by the teachings of Hippocrates, a doctor who lived during the Peloponnesian War. Unlike other doctors of his time, Hippocrates did not believe that illness and disease could be treated with magic or witchcraft. Instead, he believed that sickness had natural causes that could be cured with natural treatments. Hippocrates, often called the father of medicine, may have written as many as 80 works on sickness and medical treatments. Today, most new doctors still take the Hippocratic Oath, a pledge to provide patients with the best care possible.

out again." According to modern-day doctors, the symptoms Thucydides described do not exactly fit any disease known today. Based on Thucydides' writings, doctors guess that the plague might have been one of two viruses—smallpox or Ebola—or typhus, which is spread by lice and fleas. Today, doctors call the unknown illness Thucydides' Syndrome.

An engraving titled The Death of Pericles, *by 19th century artist Chappel, captured the Athenian leader's final moments.*

The Great Plague took a terrible toll on Athens. Historians estimate that as many as one out of three Athenians died. One of the plague's victims

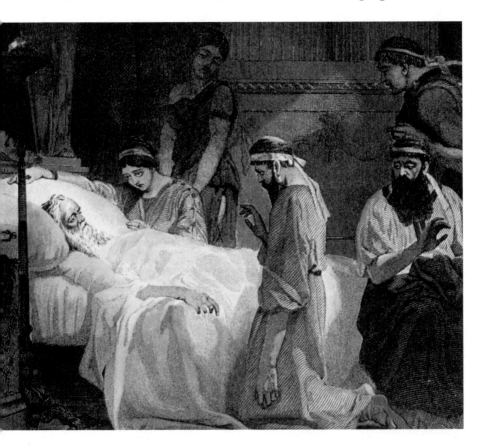

was Pericles, the city's "first citizen." The loudest voice against offensive attacks on Sparta was silenced forever.

After Pericles' death, two men came to prominence. One was Cleon, the opponent of Pericles and an advocate of a full-scale war with Sparta. The other was Nicias, who, unlike Cleon, was a dignified and cautious man. However, he also favored continuing the war. Together, the two began planning a counterattack against their enemy.

Although the city had been weakened by the plague, the people refused to give up the fight against Sparta. In June 428, the Athenian navy and army began making attacks on Sparta. They also forced rebellious former allies, like the city of Mytilene on the island of Lesbos, into obedience.

In his writing, Thucydides took great interest in recording the technical details of land and sea battles. His battle scenes include soldiers' feelings of excitement, fear, and despair. He wrote about

After the defeat of Mytilene, Cleon proposed that all of Mytilene's adult males be executed and the women and children be sold as slaves. After some discussion, the assembly agreed. A ship was immediately sent to carry out the plan. But the following day the Athenians had second thoughts, and another ship was sent to stop the execution. In order to catch the first ship, the crew rowed while they ate and took turns sleeping. Thucydides wrote, "The first [ship] arrived so little before them that [the general] had only just time ... to prepare to execute the sentence, when the second ... prevented the massacre. The danger of Mytilene had indeed been great."

withstanding sieges, fighting in the mountains, battling barbarians, and attacking enemy fleets. Many of the land battles were fought the same way they had been 200 years earlier. The army was made up of hoplites, soldiers protected by heavy armor. Each hoplite carried a shield and spear.

Battles were usually fought in the daytime, with one side facing the other. Each army's hoplites banded together in a phalanx, a fighting formation in which the soldiers stood in rows of eight or 16 with their shields joined together and their spears overlapped. The side that had the better, stronger

In battles during the fourth century B.C., the Macedonian army also used the phalanx formation.

army won. A war was often over after one battle.

During the Peloponnesian War, however, the approach to battle began to change. Thucydides, being a fighting man himself, was very interested in these changes. Each side used mercenaries, or paid soldiers, to fight for them. Other new strategies included the use of lightly armed troops for greater speed and new formations to surprise the enemy.

In 425, Cleon's army used new tactics to defeat the Spartans at Sphacteria, an island in the Ionian Sea. Thucydides described the effect the Athenian strategy had on the battle:

> They [the Athenians] now rushed upon them all together with loud shouts and pelted them with stones, darts, and arrows, whichever came first hand. The shouting accompanying their onset confounded the Spartans, unaccustomed to this mode of fighting; dust rose from the newly burnt wood, and it was impossible to see in front of one with the arrows and stones flying through the clouds of dust ... they themselves [the Spartans] were unable to retaliate, being prevented from using their eyes to see what was before them, and unable to

Cleon's victory at Sphacteria was a shocking and humiliating defeat for the Spartans. Even the Athenians and their allies were amazed. Thucydides wrote, "It was the general opinion that no force or famine could make the Spartans give up their arms, but that they would fight on as they could, and die with them in their hands: indeed people could scarcely believe that those who had surrendered were of the same stuff as the fallen."

hear the words of command for the hubbub raised by the enemy.

After the Athenian victory, the Spartans realized that the war would be long and messy. They asked the

Athenians for peace. In Book III, Thucydides recorded their words:

> *It is not reasonable ... for you to think that, because of your present strength ... fortune will always be on your side. True wisdom is shown by those who make careful use of their advantages in the knowledge that things will change. ... Now is the time to be reconciled while the issue is undecided and you can acquire glory and our friendship and we can be relieved from our distress before anything shameful has happened.*

But Cleon refused to accept the peace offer. He hated Sparta and wanted to destroy the proud city. He also hoped to expand the Athenian empire. After the Athenians rejected the Spartan peace proposal, Cleon returned to Sphacteria and defeated the Spartan soldiers who had taken shelter there. According to Thucydides, the Athenian general brought 292 prisoners of war back to Athens with him as hostages. ☙

7 THE END OF A CAREER

❧❧❧

In 424 B.C., when Thucydides was in his 30s, he was elected *strategos*, or general. The office of strategos was an important one and the only one not chosen by lot. Instead, the people of Athens selected 10 men each year to serve. Usually, only upper-class Athenians were chosen as generals. Men who did their jobs well could be reelected year after year.

Generals had to be capable of commanding Athens' armed forces. They did more than just command the navy and army, however. Because they were often stationed far from Athens, they were expected to make important decisions and act independently. They sometimes negotiated or signed treaties with foreign states, although the treaties always needed to be ratified by Athens' assembly.

Alcibiades was depicted as a general who was motivated by greed in Thucydides' history.

Like other Athenian generals, Thucydides had to answer to the Athenian assembly. Each year, the generals reported to the assembly at least 10 times. If they made mistakes or misused their power, they could be removed from office and banished.

During wartime, the role of general became especially important. Wartime generals were given specific commands and operations to carry out. Because of his ties to Thrace, Thucydides was given command of the northern naval fleet. His headquarters were in Eion, a town three miles (4.8 km) south of Amphipolis.

In December, Thucydides received an urgent plea for help from the nearby Athenian colony of

Greek warships featured three tiers of oars on each side.

Amphipolis. The brilliant Spartan general Brasidas had made surprise attacks on Athenian allies in northeastern Greece. Word came that he was moving swiftly toward the important port town of Amphipolis.

Thucydides was not in Eion when the message came, however. Instead, he was in Thasos, a half-day's sail away. When Thucydides learned of the danger, he rushed to Amphipolis, but he arrived too late. With the help of traitors in the town, Brasidas had taken control of Amphipolis just hours before Thucydides arrived. Of all Athens' losses during the war, the capture of the port colony was one of the most devastating. All over Thrace, cities began rebelling against Athenian rule.

Having failed in his mission, Thucydides went into exile. Historians are unsure where Thucydides lived while he was in exile from Athens. According to one account written after his death, he may have returned to his estate in Thrace, the land of his ancestors.

The town of Eion in Thrace was chosen as the headquarters of the Athenian northern fleet for its important location at the mouth of the Strymon River, just south of Amphipolis. The city had been captured from the Persians in 476 B.C. After the capture of Amphipolis, Thucydides was able to successfully defend Eion against Brasidas and the Spartan army before going into exile. Despite their importance in ancient times, the two Thracian cities no longer exist. Today, Amphipolis lies in ruins, and the exact location of what was once Eion is unknown.

Although banished from his homeland, Thucydides was allowed to travel as long as he didn't return to Athens.

Thucydides took advantage of this allowance. He devoted his time to recording the Peloponnesian War. He made many contacts during the course of the war and was especially interested in talking to

Brasidas was a bold and charming leader for Sparta.

men who had fought in the battles. Thucydides wanted to hear their tales of victories, losses, and bloodshed. As an exile, he was able to talk to Athenians and their Peloponnesian enemies. In this way, he heard both sides of the story.

Thucydides was not the only general who failed to rescue Amphipolis. In 422, a final bloody battle for the town was fought. During the conflict, which Athens lost, both Cleon and Brasidas were killed.

After the death of Brasidas in 422, the people of Amphipolis honored their one-time conqueror as a hero. The citizens built a monument to the Spartan and adopted him as the city's founder, replacing the actual Athenian founder of the town. Each year, they held athletic games in his honor and made sacrifices in his memory.

With both generals gone, many people in Athens and Sparta who opposed the war saw a golden opportunity to make peace. In Athens, Nicias became the strongest voice in the assembly. According to Thucydides, Nicias hoped to be known "as a man who had never done harm to his city." In 421, the Peace of Nicias brought a temporary halt to the war.

The Peace of Nicias was meant to last for 50 years. But by 415 a new voice—Alcibiades—demanded a return to war. He was an outspoken and showy man who wanted to expand the Athenian empire. Thucydides recognized both good and bad qualities in the man. Alcibiades was a brilliant military leader. A wealthy man, he loved the good things in life,

For a time, Alcibiades was treated like a hero in Athens.

especially the prize-winning horses that he kept for chariot races.

But like Cleon, Alcibiades could also be cruel.

In 416, during peace with Sparta, the Athenians decided to conquer Melos, an independent island in the Aegean Sea. When the island finally surrendered, Alcibiades proposed killing the men and enslaving the women and children on the island. The Athenian assembly agreed.

A year later, Alcibiades convinced the Athenians to invade Sicily, an island in the Mediterranean. In Book VI, Thucydides wrote that by leading the attack on the island, Alcibiades hoped to become wealthier. The Athenian general aspired to conquer Carthage, a city on the north coast of Africa.

The expedition to Sicily set off in June 415. Thucydides described it as "the most expensive and glorious armament coming from a single city with a purely Greek force that put to sea up to that time."

The fleet included 134 triremes, or Greek warships, as well as troop ships carrying more than 5,000 hoplites. In Sicily, the Athenian generals decided to sail into the harbor of Syracuse, a Corinthian city on the east coast. This hostile

During Thucydides' time, Carthage was known for its immense wealth and power. The city was founded during the seventh century B.C. by the Phoenicians, ancient people who lived in modern-day Lebanon, Syria, and Israel. Carthage amassed a vast empire by taking control of parts of North Africa and southern Spain, as well as the islands of Sardinia, Corsica, and the western half of Sicily. The city was destroyed in 146 B.C. at the end of the Punic Wars with Rome.

A 19th-century illustration of the naval battle at Syracuse, which ended the Peace of Nicias

act amounted to a declaration of war. The Peace of Nicias, meant to last half a century, was finished. It had barely lasted six years.

Back home in Athens, the people had turned against Alcibiades. Thucydides wrote that "his activities in his private life offended everyone." The historian reported that Alcibiades ran up heavy debts, and other historians accused him of treating his wife badly and being hot-tempered, vain, and outspoken. One accusation he faced was of vandalizing statues of the god Hermes. Shortly after he set sail with the navy, Alcibiades was tried by the assembly back in

Athens and sentenced to death.

Before the sentence could be carried out, Alcibiades fled to Sparta, where he offered his services. Thucydides reported a speech Alcibiades made to convince the Spartans of his usefulness:

> *If I did you great harm as an enemy, I could likewise do you good service as a friend, inasmuch as I know the plans of the Athenians, while I only guessed yours.*

Thucydides offered an explanation of why Alcibiades turned against his own people. "I do not consider that I am now attacking a city that is still mine; I am rather trying to recover one that is mine no longer," Alcibiades told the Spartans.

With Alcibiades gone, Nicias was forced to lead Athens' army in a war he hadn't wanted. Although he was a good and honest politician, Nicias was a failure as a general. Over a two-year period, he watched as his navy and army were slowly wiped out. To make matters worse, the Spartans now invaded Attica and built a permanent fort 14 miles (22.4 km) northeast of Athens. People living in the countryside were once again forced to take shelter behind Athens' walls. The Spartans blocked trade routes and prevented supplies from reaching Athens. Defeat seemed inevitable for the Athenians. ℘

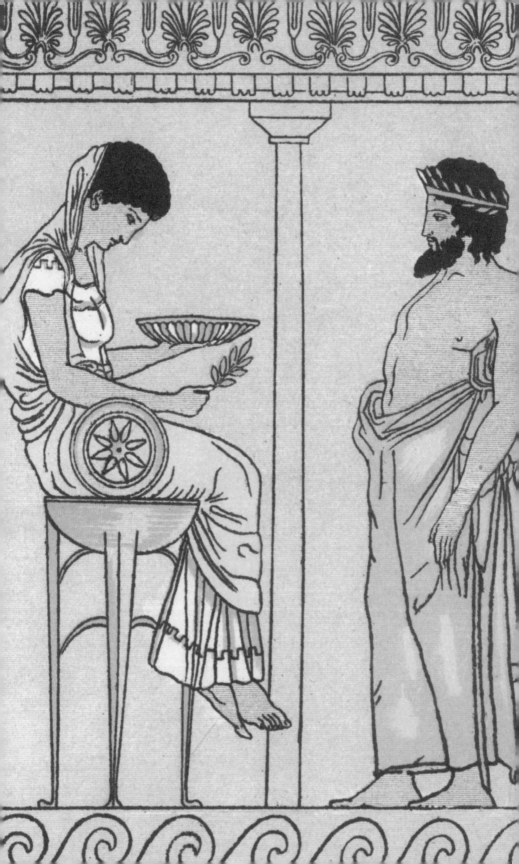

8 A DISASTROUS EXPEDITION

❧❧❧

Book VII of Thucydides' history covers just two years, 414 and 413 B.C. In 414, the war had been dragging on for 18 long years. By the summer of 413, Nicias was ready to accept defeat and leave Syracuse in retreat back to Athens. Although such an action would be shameful, it would save what was left of his navy and army. On the night of August 27, however, the Athenians witnessed a total eclipse of the moon. The men were frightened. What could this strange event mean?

An oracle warned Nicias that the eclipse was a bad omen. He recommended that Nicias wait for several weeks before leaving. The Athenian general took the advice and refused to return to Athens. The decision proved disastrous.

A Greek leader consults an oracle in search of guidance in a detail of a Greek vase painting.

The Syracusan and Spartan soldiers over-powered the Athenians.

The Syracusans, with help from Spartan soldiers, soon defeated the Athenians. In early September, Nicias and his men were surrounded and forced to surrender. Syracuse's assembly voted to execute Nicias and another Athenian general, and they were both put to death. Thucydides wrote:

Of all the Greeks, in my time, at any rate, he least deserved to meet with such extreme misfortune because he had led his entire life in accordance with virtue.

The defeat of Nicias and the Athenian military was a stunning blow to the citizens of Athens. They tried to understand how such a disaster could have happened. Many remembered other evil omens and signs that had led priests and oracles to warn against such a campaign. Some Athenians blamed the defeat on their leaders' refusal to pay attention to these bad omens.

Thucydides disagreed. He did not believe that success or failure was the result of the wishes of the gods or fate. He wrote, "We usually blame chance for whatever does not happen as we expected." Instead, he thought the decisions made by men caused the Athenian failure. For example, Nicias' decision to remain too long in Syracuse cost the general the war and his life.

Thucydides' view of religion was very different from his fellow Greeks. At that time, most Greeks believed that events in their world

Each god had different strengths and qualities. For example, the Greek god Poseidon ruled the seas. Zeus was the king of all gods. The Greeks believed that the gods, often disguised as humans, came down from Mount Olympus and interacted with their subjects. In addition, each city-state worshipped its own patron god. The patron god was thought to watch over and protect the city. Athens' patron god was Athena, goddess of wisdom and war. Sparta's patron god was Ares, the god of war.

Zeus ruled over all the Greek gods.

were controlled or directed by the 12 major gods and goddesses that lived on Mount Olympus.

In order for Greeks to understand what the gods wanted from them, they visited oracles who lived in shrines around Greece. The oracles—supposedly using special powers—relayed wishes, instructions, commands, and displeasure from the gods. They sometimes looked into the future and made predictions. Thucydides didn't believe that the oracles had any part in making or shaping history, apart from changing the behavior of the people who believed in them. For example, in Book I, Thucydides talks about how one Athenian, Cylon, may have started a failed rebellion after misinterpreting the prophecy from an oracle.

The Athenians were likely hoping the gods would now look upon them with favor. Their defeat in Sicily wiped out the city-state's navy and army. Those who survived were held captive in a stone quarry, where most died within eight months. Thucydides said that "only a few of many came back home."

It seemed impossible for Athens to continue the war, but over the next nine years, Athens kept on fighting. As the war dragged on, Thucydides continued to work on his history. He edited and improved the early sections of his book, and he decided how to date events throughout the war. He wanted his history to record the events exactly as they happened, in order from beginning to end. At this time, however, each Greek city-state used a different calendar.

Thucydides' history mentions three different date references to the start of the war. It was his attempt to try to make this important date recognizable to non-Athenians. However, that method was not very accurate and was quite confusing. Instead of using the Athenian or any other Greek calendar, Thucydides chose to date battles and other wartime events by summers and winters. For example, the historian said that the Peace of Nicias began in the spring, just at the end of winter, in the 10th year of the war. Thucydides also

Although city-states called their months by different names, all based their calendars on the cycles of the moon and the sun. Athens' calendar, for example, started each new year with the first new moon after the summer solstice, which is the day when the sun is at its northernmost position in the sky. Because a year of 12 moons did not entirely add up to one solar year, the Greeks added an extra month to their calendar every few years to make the months line up with the changing seasons. Most of the months were named for the major gods.

mentioned eclipses, which helps modern historians accurately date events that took place thousands of years ago.

As he wrote the story of Greece's great war, Thucydides tried to remain neutral and present an unbiased view. As an Athenian citizen, this was not an easy task. Even as he traveled around Greece interviewing soldiers and leaders, Thucydides knew that eyewitnesses could themselves be biased and unreliable. He wrote:

> *And with reference to the narrative of events, far from permitting myself to derive it from the first source that came to hand, I did not even trust my own impressions, but it rests partly on what I saw myself, partly on what others saw for me, the accuracy of the report being always tried by the most severe and detailed tests possible. My conclusions have cost me some labor from the want of coincidence between accounts of the same occurrences by different eyewitnesses, arising sometimes from imperfect memory, sometimes from undue partiality for one side or the other.*

Some modern historians believe that Thucydides slanted events to show Athens in the best light possible. However, he also made an effort to point out the positive aspects of Sparta's military way of life. He described the Spartans as "both warlike and wise."

Thucydides was able to present both sides of the war because of his exile from Athens. In Thrace, he was not exposed to the patriotism and pro-Athenian views of the people. Far from Athens, he could look at events from a less biased point of view. One modern-day historian wrote, "Exile may be the making of a historian."

As he wrote, Thucydides kept in mind the work of history writers who had come before him—and he found much to criticize. One writer he discussed in his book was Hellanicus, who lived during the 400s. Hellanicus wrote about the 50-year period between the Persian and Peloponnesian wars. However, Thucydides faulted him for being inaccurate. Although he doesn't name him directly, Thucydides also seemed to criticize Herodotus, a Greek historian who believed that the Persian Wars were the most important events in Greek history. Again, Thucydides believed that Herodotus did not do

Greek historian Herodotus

A two-sided statue features the two fathers of history, Herodotus (left) and Thucydides.

enough fact-checking.

Thucydides and Herodotus had different writing styles. Like other Athenian authors, Herodotus wrote his history to be read out loud. At the time, this was the method used by the greatest writers in the world. Playwrights wrote both tragedies and comedies that were recited aloud in front of an audience. There was even a class of people, called orators, who wrote speeches to be read at trials or in the Athenian assembly.

To make sure that his listeners were entertained and amused, Herodotus included romantic side stories that had little to do with the war. He also wrote about the customs of people in other places, and he even included women in his books. Following the customs and beliefs of his fellow Athenian men, Thucydides rarely mentioned women at all.

Thucydides' writing style was much drier than that of Herodotus. He preferred to write about facts and statistics instead of emotions and myths. In some parts of his works, he included the tiniest details of battles and other events. Thucydides admitted that his stories might not be as colorful or entertaining as those of Herodotus. He wrote, "My own work may seem less enjoyable because of the absence of any element of romance."

Herodotus was born around 484 B.C. in Halicarnassus, a town located in present-day Turkey. During his lifetime, he traveled to Egypt, Athens, Persia, and all around the Mediterranean lands. Herodotus was especially interested in people's customs, religious practices, and social behavior. Unlike Thucydides, his writings included information about the society's culture. Herodotus is known for his nine books on the war between Persia and Greece. Near the end of his life, Herodotus settled in the newly founded Athenian colony of Thurii in Italy. It is believed he died toward the end of the fifth century.

However, he pointed out that the stories he told were intended as "a possession for all time."